Mount Up Your Wings

Unlock Your Inner Genius and Create Lasting Wealth

UGO MADUKA

CONTENTS

Actions

DEDICATION

To God almighty, whose grace made it possible. To my very beautiful and supportive wife Amarachi, our children Judah Chinecherem and Cyrus Jidenna Maduka, and to everyone whose lives would be forever transformed by the contents of this book.

INTRODUCTION

The ride from JFK airport was pretty smooth. It was around noon on a cold day in January. I couldn't keep my eyes off the windows, I kept observing and admiring the beautiful scenery of New York City.

Here I was, riding in a taxi in the famous *United States of America*. I had high expectations and I was pumped up with excitement.

My eyes caught sight of the winter beaten trees, the quality road routes with clearly marked lanes and ever busy intersections.

It wasn't until they dropped me off in a suburb called the Bronx that I saw a different US. A far cry from what was portrayed in Hollywood movies.

On day one of my arrival, I got the shock of my life! Right before my eyes, I saw dilapidated buildings, haggard-looking men and women sleeping on street corners, while others were begging for spare change to buy food.

Looking at these folks in their pitiful state, you could see in their eyes the pain of broken dreams and the regrets of miscalculated choices. A mix of hurt and compassion flowed through me for them.

Now don't get me wrong, the United States of America is a great place. Ever since I was a kid, I've always wanted to live in the US, particularly New York or Los Angeles. So I was shocked to the marrow to see such levels of dejection and despondence in a land that boasts of limitless opportunities for wealth creation.

I spent a few nights in New York City and decided to head out West to Los Angeles, California, the land of dreams. Surprisingly, I saw some of the same lifestyle themes in LA.

I drove past a neighborhood where sleeping tents littered street corners right beside the glitz and glamour of Hollywood, arguably the most recognized attraction in the world. I later learned that area, referred to as Skid Row, is the largest homeless encampment in the Los Angeles County.

I felt so heartbroken. The compassion flowing in my heart was not just because of where these people found themselves at the moment, but because deep within me I knew they'd have their own stories of life's failures.

They would've done better if they knew better, especially if given another chance. But then, such is life.

Standing in the midst of that despair brought me to the conclusion that poverty knows no race, color, or gender.

POVERTY IS A MINDSET. Poverty is everywhere. Anywhere around the world, the fact still remains that you can be in the midst of abundance and still be stuck in poverty.

How else can you explain the fact that in the face of the massive economic, political, technological, and socio-cultural activities taking place in California and New York, its cities still hold the highest rates of homelessness. The answer is "POVERTY MINDSET."

We can recognize that poverty exists for three basic reasons.

The first reason is an unawareness of the innate mental capacity you possess to create wealth.

This means that no matter how hard you seem to be working at the moment, if you are yet to have some sort of financial stability, you are underutilizing your productive capacity by failing to explore and tap into your creativity.

The second reason is the reckless behavior of spending more money than you earn.
Let's say you earn $3,000 per month while your expenses total $5,000 at the end of every month. You don't need anyone to tell you that you are living beyond your means and that you'll soon be swimming in debt.

The fact that you can pay for it does not mean you can afford it.

The third reason is the inability to subject yourself to the mental discipline and active process it takes to become successful and create lasting wealth.

With few exceptions for disabled persons and others who have endured tough life experiences in their journey, if you did a little digging into the history of poor people today, you would definitely see a trace or more of these three factors.

It is true that you don't get to determine certain factors surrounding your start in life. Factors like who your parents are or when and where you were born. However, in life, it is not intended that the factors outside of your control impede or hinder your progress.

Some say life is 10 percent what happens to you and 90 percent what you do about it. Whatever the ratio is, it is quite inspiring to know that the right effort in the right direction can still make a huge difference.

You may not have determined your beginning but you surely have the ability to determine how you end.

Life is all about the choices you make, as we were given the freewill to choose any path we desire. No matter the cards we were dealt, we navigate life through our choices.

While some of us actually figure it out, some keep trying, and some others are at the verge of giving up or not making any attempt at all. The difference is all in the attitude.

This book serves as a guide through the "90 percent" actions you can take to set your life on the right track.

By reading this book, you will realize that you are the major determinant of your success. You desire to end well regardless of how you started. For that, I congratulate you and welcome you into the realm of winners.

This book is inspired by many years of careful research, mentorship, and observation of the lives of great achievers, their habits, beliefs, routines, and actions.
Inside, you'll not only understand what real success is but also grasp the key ingredients necessary for the journey of success.

It would shock you to know that a lot of people are yet to understand that the journey of success in any endeavor requires careful and deliberate calculated steps.

If you want to be rich and never be broke again, your actions, habits, and daily routines must reflect that desire.

This book aims to keep you motivated and reignite your passion to maximize your drive toward becoming better and achieving more.

Whoever you are or whatever it is that you do, if your mission is to grow and become successful, you are surely on the right path with this book.

I urge you to receive this book with an open mind to unlearn and relearn; keeping in mind that no amount of time spent acquiring wisdom is considered a waste of time.

No matter who you are – an aspiring entrepreneur, an established business owner or even an employee, whatever your profession is – I believe that as you soar through the pages of this book, one or two aspects of the principles, stories and examples stated inside might resonate with you or somebody you know.

That alone can ultimately act as the catalyst or the light-bulb moment for that great idea that has been lying dormant within you.

This learning material in your hand is not just a motivational book but also a transformational business book.

Included at the end of every chapter are action steps to take for easy guidance and implementation based on the lessons and knowledge you have learned so far.

Let me assure you that if you commit to read this material to the last page and diligently apply the recommended action steps, your life will never be the same.

So, let's get it on.

CHAPTER 1

THE STARTING POINT

A young engineer was contracted to design and put up a magnificent building from scratch.

Just a few days after laying the building foundation, he went to the city water and power supply company requesting the utilities at the new site be turned on.

The utilities company visited the building site and discovered that there was no electrical infrastructure in place except for the actual building foundation.

The servicing officer of the power and water supply company in their astounded state instantly denied the engineer his request to be connected to the power grid.

They went on to explain to him that to have the flow of water and power supplied to him, his building or structure ought to already be standing with all the right piping and wiring systems in place, otherwise, there'd be a lot of wastage and chaos if they were crazy enough to oblige him.

As ridiculous as this analogy may seem, this is the reality of many adults and young people in our society today. From this example, it is easy to see why a lot of people's lives are nothing but chaotic and disorganized. They lack the basic sense of planning, preparing, and executing ideas.

For you to activate the flow of opportunities for wealth into your life, you have to put the right structures in place.

Without the right structures, you will just be running helter-skelter, deluding yourself into thinking that you are working very hard, only for you to wake up one day and you are fifty-five years old or with nothing to show for it.

One major foundational structure that has to be in place is the right mindset. This is the ability to think correctly, set higher expectations, and plan and implement strategies.

The Oxford English Dictionary defines the mind as the element of a person that enables them to be aware of the world. It is the part of your existence that enables you to think and to feel. The mind is the faculty of consciousness and thought; it is the core of your existence.

I have heard stories of people who got a promotion at work, changed jobs, or even migrated from their place of abode to go seek greener pastures elsewhere, only to end up in the same position, or even worse off and more broke than they were in the past.

What does that tell you?

A lizard can never become an alligator by just jumping into the lake. A domestic cat can never become a tiger by merely living in the jungle. There is something on the inside that makes the alligator, an alligator and the tiger, a tiger. Therefore, if you desire to change the level of your existence, something needs to change on your inside and that thing is your mindset.

Your mindset is what determines if you will be successful or not. This is because your mind births thoughts, the thoughts become actions, the actions become habits, and the habits form character.

Your character is what determines who and what you attract, and of course you already know that you are the average of the five people you hang around with.

So you see why you need to do a reappraisal of your mind so that you can get better results and live a more fulfilled life.

You might be asking, what is it about the mind? I purposely chose to make this topic the first chapter for a reason. If you want to be successful, you need to first of all assess your mentality to understand what your perception of success is.

Deconstruct And Reconstruct Your Paradigm

For you to move from being broke to becoming successful, you will have to first understand that success, whether in business or relationship, is an attitude. Your attitude is formed by your paradigm, which is the way you think about yourself and see the world around you.

Successful people have an attitude that makes them different from people who are broke. You have to learn to cultivate the same attitude as successful people.

To do this, you will have to deconstruct and reconstruct your paradigm. You do this by asking yourself critical questions such as why are you the way you are? Why do you reason in a certain way? What do you fear most? Why do you fear it?

The answers you get will help you to unlearn and relearn some, if not all, of the things you've been taught about wealth, success, and relationships your whole life.

Unlearning here does not just mean changing your beliefs and your behavior. It involves reevaluating your sources of information, your biased orientation, and letting go of your old thought patterns because they are obviously not working for you.

It's a good thing you found this book, so let's go do some deconstruction and reconstruction.

i. Limiting beliefs

In the animal kingdom, the lion is said to be the king of the jungle. The lion is not the tallest animal. The giraffe is way taller. It is neither the fattest nor the heaviest compared to the hippos, rhinos, and elephants. The lion is not the fastest, neither the smartest nor the most intelligent, yet, it is king.

What makes the lion unique is its attitude. The lion has an attitude that draws a lot of respect from other animals. All animals fear and respect the lion, and you wonder, what makes these fierce and larger animals fear the lion?

The answer is its attitude and mindset.

No matter how big or intelligent you are or how many degree certificates you possess, if you think lowly of yourself, you will always be limited in your achievements.

It is what you think in your mind that keeps you small.

Conversely, it also doesn't matter how small or young you are, how unintelligent people may perceive you to be, or how much you don't have at the moment. It's your thinking that makes the difference.

Successful people think differently and this leads them to behave in certain ways that stretch them beyond the limitations of societal norms and expectations. It is a person's thinking that makes them see circumstances differently.

Attitude as we already know is embedded in beliefs. What you believe about yourself determines your attitude. Your attitude determines your actions and your actions determine your results.

You don't have to be a certain height, hold a certain degree, or be a certain race, tribe or shape to be successful. It is your attitude, which stems from the beliefs you hold in your mind, that determines whether you'll be successful or broke.

ii. Small thinkers

A man went out one day to fish in his beautiful little boat at the community lake. He arrived at the lake and met a couple of other fishermen spread out in different parts of the lake.

After several hours of attempts and no catch, he resolved to proceed home. As he was going to return his boat back to shore, he looked up and noticed not too far off from his boat some of the fishermen he'd met earlier when he first arrived, throwing fishes back into the lake.

Out of curiosity, he approached the men to find out the reason for such a display of foolishness according to his reasoning.

"Sir, I noticed you and your friend have been returning most of your catch back into the water," he said. "Do you mind me asking why?" he continued.

The two men looked at each other and with great glee one of them replied, "Well, we like to fry our fish full length, and so we came out here with a piece of wood, the size of our skillet at home."

"We simply measure the fish with the length of the stick, and if the fish is longer than the stick, we already know that it won't fit into our pan, so, we throw it back into the water," he concluded excitedly.

The story above is an example of what limitation, mediocrity, or a small mindset can bring about.

I can almost feel you say "what morons" but the sad reality is that a lot of people are just like these two ignorant fishermen, only in their case, their own little frying pan is their small mind.

You, like a lot people, are afraid to dream big and aspire to be more. This fear can be directly traced to your attitude that has been shaped by several factors such as family background, environmental influence, peer groups, societal expectations, and spiritual and psychological myths you've been programmed into.

Did you know that most of the perceptions you hold about yourself are not the true reflection of what you carry on your inside? You are just a victim of other people's assessment and judgment of you.

Just like the two fishermen mentioned earlier, how many great ideas have you blocked out because of your small frying pan of a mind?

You are simply unable to attract and retain the bigger fish of ideas because your mind is not programmed or wired for the bigger opportunities. You are afraid to step out in courage and take more risks.

You'd rather play it safe and remain a local champion.

iii. Visualization.

I was told the story of a young man who lived in one of the suburbs of New York, about 45 minutes driving distance from Manhattan. What struck me about his story and makes it worth referencing here is that he said that in his over thirty-five years of existence, he had never been to Manhattan. According to him, he had no reason to go there.

For those who don't know Manhattan, it is among the world's major commercial, financial, and cultural centers. It is where you have the Empire State Building, Times Square, and many other big buildings and skyscrapers.

Ordinarily, you might not see anything wrong with his choice, but in the context of this discussion, everything is wrong with it.

Here you have a man, who's struggling to get by, lives in a single room apartment, and is battling to make more money, but has never stepped outside of his environment. How then can he be inspired?

Visualization is the formation of a mental image of something or a situation.
Compare your mind to a garden of some sort. Just like it is with a real garden, you need to consistently protect, cultivate, and plant good seeds in your garden.

Failure to do so creates room for unwanted rodents, pests, and weeds to naturally invade and grow there.

Therefore, it is very important that you take out time every day to visualize your future by learning how to see yourself already living the life you desire in your head.

Your life is what you think it should be. Whether you believe it or not, your current state is exactly what you thought into existence.

My life is proof of this fact.

Right from my childhood days, I've always dreamed and talked about living in the United States.

Today, that dream has become a reality.

If you don't like who you are at the moment, you've got to change the way you think by visualizing yourself differently.

Exposing your eyes to objects, places, and visions of wealth, for instance with magazines, vacations, car showrooms, and so forth, is a good way to start.

This is what the law of attraction is all about. You attract what you think about the most. This is not a mystery or some feel-good psychotherapy, but a product of your mind's programming.

Compare that to the story of renowned TV and radio personality Steve Harvey, who said that when he was a kid, his parents though they were poor, understood the power of painting mental pictures.

He said his father was too broke to take them on vacations, but his mother would always bring home travel magazines with pictures of exotic locations and luxury items.

Whenever his father asked her why she always spent money on such items, she said, "We don't have money to take this boy nowhere, but if he can look into these magazines, maybe one day it would make him want to travel."

Steve said he has been to several countries and cities, not necessarily for work but just to go see stuff. Why? Because of the pictures he drew from those magazines.

He went on to say that during Christmas time, his father would drive them in his car from the hood where they lived to the suburbs and city centers so they could see the Christmas lights, which did fascinate him a lot.

He said something else caught his attention and made him curious. According to him, most of the big houses in the suburbs had horseshoe driveways. The type that you drive in through one end and pull out through the other end, nothing like the tiny parking space they were used to in the hood.

Steve said that he was so fascinated with these driveway designs that he had to ask his father why they couldn't get one. His father replied and said to him, "Boy, I don't have the money to afford one, but that's why I'm bringing you out here to see them, so that one day you'll be able to get one of these houses."

Now, Steve said he's owned about eleven homes in his lifetime and every one of them has that horseshoe driveway. Talk about the power of painting mental pictures.

The good thing about painting mental pictures is that it broadens your mind, making you aspire and desire more. So feed your mind with the right images by thinking good thoughts.

Where you will be in the next five or ten years will be determined by your thought patterns today. This leads me to my next point, which is the words that proceed from your mouth.

iv. What are you telling yourself?

Another important aspect of mindset shift to examine is what you are telling yourself at any given moment. What conversation are you having with yourself? What do you say to yourself, when things don't go the way you planned them?

As humans, there is a natural inclination to want to put yourself down, especially after a bad experience. But you need to train your mind and your mouth to speak positively.

What you don't know is that words are powerful energies that are most potent when you are emotionally charged up.

It's just like the Miranda Warning, issued by the police at the point of arrest. Whatever you say at that point might make or break you. Whatever negative words you speak in that emotionally charged up state will always come back to haunt you in the future.

The Bible in the Book of Proverbs chapter 23 verse 7 KJV version says, "As a man thinketh, so is he."

Whatever negative thoughts you constantly reenact in your mind and continually tell yourself over time begin to seem believable.

You somehow start seeing them to be true and the more you believe them, the more they manifest themselves.

Action Steps

1. Never be afraid to dream big; dream dreams so big that they intimidate you.

2. No matter how big you are, how intelligent you are, how many degrees you've got, if you think lowly of yourself, you will always be limited in your achievements. It is what you think in your mind that keeps you small.

Conversely, it also doesn't matter how small or young you are, how unintelligent people may perceive you to be, or how much you don't have at the moment, it's your thinking that makes you successful.

3. Words are powerful energies; always speak positive words to yourself, no matter the circumstance, the universe is always listening.

CHAPTER
2

MAKING CHOICES

One Wrong Choice, Many Years Of Pain And Regret

One of my close friends shared a touching story with me about his rough teenage years growing up in Grand Rapids, Michigan.

Grand Rapids is a somewhat a big city, with its own share of activities. Although nothing compared to the state of New York in terms of the lifestyle, it's still got that mix of the good, the bad, and the ugly.

Kevin told me how he was always engaged in one street fight or the other every day with a very close buddy of his called Mike.

He said it was so bad that no day passed without some random parent or neighbor showing up at their house to complain to his father about their misdemeanors.

Whenever his dad confronted him about the reports, his reply was always that they came at him. "They came looking for my trouble," he'd say.

According to him, one afternoon as he was dressed up to go out, his dad who was watching

TV in the living room inquired where he was going.

He said he was going to hang out with his friend Mike. His dad just smiled and invited him to come sit down and watch TV with him instead.

Reluctantly, he obeyed and slouched into one of the couches in the room and before he knew it, dozed off.

He woke up some three hours later to the smiling face of his dad. "Did anyone come looking for your trouble today?" his dad asked rhetorically.

Though he did not give any answer, the lesson was clear. According to him, that day marked a turning point in his life. Every evening, his dad would invite him to sit in with him and watch TV or they'd review the day's newspapers together.

By this act, he started hanging out less with his friend Mike and also improved in his knowledge and reading skills.

Meanwhile, Mike's parents tried to adopt the same disciplinary strategy of keeping him indoors but he would have none of it. He was just too stubborn for them to handle.

They tried to enforce stricter rules on him but it wasn't working. He thought his parents were being needlessly overbearing and "meddling too much in his business," he would argue.

It got so bad that Mike decided to move out of his parent's house to go live with some of his older friends who were already living in their own apartment on the other side of town.

How sweet the taste of freedom, he thought to himself. As the years went by, my friend Kevin graduated from high school and went on to college, while his friend dropped out of high school, continued in his thuggish ways and became a full-fledged, notorious street gangster.

I came in one day to meet Kevin in tears and upon inquiry, he told me his childhood friend Mike was dead.

Information had it that it was a robbery incident gone wrong, Mike and two other guys had gone to rob a store at gunpoint, but luck ran out on them when a team of police officers on patrol nearby engaged them in a shoot-out.

Mike was hit by a bullet in the chest and he died on the spot, while the other two guys sustained gunshot wounds.

Today, Kevin is happily married with two children and has a fledging job in the financial sector, while his friend Mike is no more.

Two friends, two choices, different paths. Kevin chose to submit himself to the authority of his parents while Mike chose otherwise and sadly faced the severe consequence in the future.

Had Mike stayed back home, had he not run away, he would never have met those dangerous friends, he would never have become an armed robber and he would still be alive today.

No matter who you are or what your age is, choice-making is personal. It is never easy to convince people to do what they don't feel in their guts to do especially when you are dealing with young people.

Interestingly, the younger you are, the more significantly the choices you make affect your future, in a good or bad way.

Like roads that lead in different directions to different locations, your choices set you in a particular direction that will eventually lead to a destination. A happy ending or a tragic one.

Like tiny little seeds with the potential of becoming great trees, little choices have potentially great consequences.

One wrong choice, no matter how insignificant or harmless it may seem, can lead you down the path of regret and many years of pain.

You may not be able to change your destination in one day, but you can surely change your direction by the sum of your daily choices multiplied over time.

Whether you believe it or not, your life as it is now, is a consequence of the choices you have made. Consciously or unconsciously, knowingly or unknowingly, all of your actions and inactions are part of the choices you made.

Success or failure is never a one-day event that happens overnight. It happens as a result of the accumulation of correctness or errors in your choices repeated every day and multiplied over time.

You don't suddenly wake up one day and find yourself rich, broke, divorced, or overweight. It was the direction you went in that got you where you are today.

Your path to failure or success is directly impacted by the choices you make every day.

On a daily basis in your life, critical decisions and choices are made. These decisions, as little or minor as they may seem at the time you make them, form the major structures of your personal development and the paths of your sojourn through life.

If you are familiar with spherical shapes like soccer or golf balls, you would know that to drive a ball toward a particular direction you would have to hit the ball at the correct angle of impact so that the ball is set on the right trajectory.

For example, if you play pool or snooker as it is called in some places, you'd know that to pot a ball into a particular hole or pocket, you would have to hit the white ball at a specific angle to get the right trajectory toward the desired hole.

Any slight shift off of the correct angle at the point of impact would send the ball shooting in another direction.

Your choices are like the impacts on that ball. The right choices made at the right time will send you down the path of fulfillment, while your wrong choices leave you with nothing but wasted years of pain and regret.

This chapter aims to shed light on your decision-making mechanisms with the hope that you begin to understand and pay more attention to the choices you make.

What that means is if you can actually begin to closely monitor and control your process of making choices, you will have better control of your life. Almost instantly, you will begin to notice and enjoy the peace of mind and liberty that comes from being in charge of yourself based on the right choices you have made.

Choices, especially poor choices, are one of the leading causes of poverty. A lot of times in trying to break out of the poverty cycle, people seem to focus on their circumstance instead of checking their choice-making process.

This behavior can be likened to a doctor focusing on symptoms instead of diagnosing the root cause of a disease.

Imagine a man with a punctured tire who instead of replacing or fixing the hole in the tire prefers a regular air refill of the damaged tire. As expected, the tire will continue to lose air again and again.

As long as you keep making wrong choices with your time, money, and in your relationships, you will always be broke and unhappy.

This same analogy is very similar to your actions when it comes to building success and wealth. If you continue to assuage and mask the symptoms instead of dealing with your problem of choice, you will never succeed. You only end up doing the same things and making the same mistakes over and over again.

If you are not where you want to be financially, if you are not living the luxurious lifestyle you've always visualized and dreamed of, the problem lies in your choices.

Think of it this way, your daily activities influenced by choice multiplied by time bring you to your long-term results.

Your circumstances are simply the symptoms of your choices.

It is one thing to think of success, yet it is another to make a choice to be determined and motivated to see it manifest into reality.

It is the accumulation of your many choices that metamorphose into a patterned process that begets a lifestyle – the kind of lifestyle that brings about financial independence.

Choice As a Catalyst

A fully developed oak tree is always thicker at the base while the branches that extend upward are thinner.

When the tree is just sprouting, the stems are so soft and light that you can easily replant it or bend it without breaking them.

When it is fully developed, with the thick stem fully formed, it is hard to bend. In fact any attempt to do so would result in breaking the tree. The best you can do is trim or hem the branches.

The same thing applies to the choices you make when you are younger. When they have formed into a habit or led you down a certain path in your later years, it is always very hard to make adjustments.

Choices are the catalysts of your future circumstances, destructively or constructively.

All of the tiny pieces of your life are very much interwoven by the cumulative consequence of your choices. Every one of them: your actions, inactions, beliefs, disbeliefs, perceptions, misconceptions, and so on.

If you are not happy with where you are today, blame it on the choices you've made from your past to your present. You are by your action or inaction, exactly the way you have chosen to be.

In the 1997 blockbuster movie *Titanic*, right before the ship's collision with an iceberg, the ship's crew had received several warnings about iceberg sightings on the high sea.

As a precautionary measure, the captain positioned some crew members atop the ship as lookouts while the ship powered on through the night.

Somewhere in the middle of the voyage, the crew members who were supposed to be on the lookout got distracted by the sight of Rose and Jack, the main characters, making out in a corner of the ship while it moved toward a gigantic iceberg at a rapid speed.

By the time they snapped out of their voyeuristic behavior, it was too late. The ship was already too close to the massive iceberg.

They blew their whistles and rang the emergency bells to alert the captain.

The captain in a swift reaction reduced steam, turned off the engine, and began to steer the ship away from the iceberg.

He steered the helm to the very last angle but it was already too late. The captain was able to avoid a head-on collision quite all right but not without the iceberg scraping the base and causing serious damage that sank the ship moments later.

Had the lookouts not chosen to allow themselves to get distracted, they would have sighted the iceberg on time. An early sighting would have required a slight turn of the helm and the ship would have completely changed course from proceeding toward the iceberg.

In life, choices are like the steering wheel of that ship. The older you get, the more difficult it is and the more effort you require to make certain changes and adjustments.

At some point in our adult lives, we all definitely come to a rude awakening that we are the architects of our destinies. We realize that our success is not dependent on anybody but ourselves.

However, what you do after this realization is a matter of choice.

The realization is not to castigate you but to propel you into making a conscious choice to do better in developing yourself and increasing your personal value.

Personally, it took me over twenty-five years of my life to begin to acknowledge and accept the consequence of my choices over the years.

If you undertake a reflection on your past, you will clearly see all the things you failed to do and the wrong choices you made.

You chose to waste time with frivolities instead of pursuing personal development. You chose to watch too much TV. You chose to hangout every evening instead of learning a valuable skill with your free time.

You chose to let your friends choose you, instead of you choosing them. You chose to settle for a meager salary as an employee instead of starting a business.

There's so much more, but so far you can now see how all of these choices and so many more influenced your life to this point.

Your broke circumstance at this moment is not because you are dim-witted or have bad luck, it is just as a result of the bad choices you have made.

The questions to ask yourself are "Where am I today?" and "How did I get here?"

If you are broke or a failure in a particular area such as marriage or relationships with others, set about this deep introspection again and ask yourself what you chose to do or not do repeatedly every day that brought you to this failure.

Your willingness to accept responsibility that your failure is a consequence of your choices over the years and make necessary adjustments will surely lead you down the path of success.

Again, choices are so powerful that even when you choose not to make a choice, it is a form of choice-making.

If at the time you are reading this book, you are below age thirty, count yourself lucky because you are still in your formative years.

What it means is that there is still time for you to easily make some major adjustments in your life. That is not to say that you still can't make effective choices when you are over age forty or more.

There is no doubt that you can, but keep in mind that it will you take you extra efforts and hard work compared to what it would have if you were younger.

It takes a slight swerve of the steering wheel to avoid collision with an object if spotted on time. But a late detection of the obstacle will have you swinging dangerously wide to avoid a collision.

The Components of Choice

When it comes to choice-making, there are no circumventions. The more right choices you make, the better your chances of becoming successful. A life of disciplined, persistent and consistent action is the core requirement for being successful more than any other aspect of being.

These core requirements are heavily dependent on the choices you make. Remember, we already mentioned that whether you take actions or not, you are still making vital choices that will vastly shape your future.

In four simple steps, here is a breakdown of the components of human choice.

1. The choice to stay idle

2. The choice to give up

3. The choice to be mediocre

4. The choice to be extra committed

Interestingly, in all your daily activities you are adopting all four of these choice-making processes but in response to different aspects of your life.

For example, you might be extra committed to a particular hobby of yours but choose to be average when it comes to your career.

Another person might be extra committed to an unprofitable, time-wasting habit like playing video games but choose to give up or even do nothing when it comes to learning about success.

You will only do best in the aspects of your life in which you choose to invest the most attention and take the most action even if the activities are non-profitable in any way.

Action Steps

1. Whether you believe it or not, your life as it is now, is a consequence of the choices you have made, consciously and unconsciously, knowingly and unknowingly; therefore, you have to be deliberate about making the right choices.

2. One wrong choice, no matter how insignificant or harmless it may seem can lead you down the path of many regrets and years of pain.

3. The younger you are, the easier it is to make choices that are more impactful.

4. The choice to be extra committed guarantees the right result for success.

CHAPTER 3

HOW TO BE A PROBLEM SOLVER

(ACTIVATE YOUR SELLING POINT)

Around 1922 and 1923, during the First World War, the German government was hit with series of debts and incessant strikes by it workers.

While trying to find a solution, instead of seeking to increase their production output, they chose a seemingly easier way by deciding to print more currency, which resulted in hyperinflation.

The hyperinflation was so bad that it rendered the German Mark, which was the currency at that time, useless.

Citizens received their wages in stacks of cash loaded up in wheelbarrows and large boxes.

The situation was so bad that some artisans like cobblers preferred food to cash in exchange for their services.

Most interesting was the story of a man who had received his wages and on his way home, had stopped briefly by a roadside store to make inquiries.

He came back outside to see that somebody had stolen his wheelbarrow, leaving behind his stacks of cash piled up in a rough heap.

The wheelbarrow held more value to the thief than the stack of cash.

Typically, in trying to be successful, a lot focus and emphasis seem to be placed on money. Don't get me wrong, money is very important, but in the context of the point I'm trying to make here, money is just what it is, a stack of paper with pictures of dead people on it.

In fact, only about 9 percent of the world's money is in cash form. What does that tell you?

The real value of money is not in a currency. Currency only has value because it is an exchange medium that people understand and accept as such and can lose its value at any time as a result of a change in government policy or war situation.

For you to be successful, there has to be something you are doing for others or a problem you are helping them solve and getting paid for it.

That thing in business terms is known as your *selling point*.

Every one you see working in organized establishments whether private or public has a selling point – a value they possess and exchange for money.

Do you ever wonder why somebody earns $10 an hour, another makes $1,000 an hour, while some others make a whopping $10,000 to $100,000 an hour?

Some people might attribute such a feat to luck, but the truth is that you don't get paid for the hour. You are paid for the value you bring to the hour. You get paid for the value of your selling points and the problem you help others solve.

The world only rewards efficiency and creativity, no matter what your race, tribe, or color is.

A smart repetition of the pattern over a period of time can generate more money and accumulate wealth for you if properly harnessed and managed.

What is Your Selling Point?

Now that you understand the concept of a selling point, my question to you is what is your selling point?

Simply put, for the purpose of this book, your selling point is the value you possess in skills or product that you can exchange for money.

You need to understand that people don't just want to throw their hard-earned money around. They want to spend their money on things of value, things that solve problems for them.

Therefore, to be a problem solver, you have to activate your selling point.
For this to happen, there has to be something you are selling, a product or some service you are rendering – something of value that you can sell or market in exchange for money.

Back in the day, before the introduction of currency into the African economic system, the medium of exchange for goods and services was the barter system.
Each household had a trademark or specific skill they possessed. They were mostly fishermen, farmers, artisans, and craftspeople.

So, for example, if you were a fisherman and you needed grains, what you would do is that you take some extra of what you have, which is fish, and proceed to the market place on a specific market day. There you would find somebody with grains who is also in need of fish and then exchange your fish for grains.

The same thing happens with the furniture maker. If he needs food in his household, he simply looks for a farmer who needs his product or service as a furniture maker and exchange goods with him.

Now this system was not limited to the exchange of goods for goods only. Sometimes, people rendered services for food too. For instance, you could offer to assist a fisherman to sea or a farmer to go harvest crops. At the end of the day, the farmer or fisherman would give you a certain portion of the day's proceeds.

This was the way of life back then. The people survived and were happy. Although, some of the major snags of the barter system were that it was time-consuming.
To get what you needed, you had to find one who had what you needed and that person also had to need what you have to offer, which caused a lot of delay in transactions.

Sometimes it took days to find the perfect transaction. It was also difficult to measure value and units. For instance, it was difficult to determine exactly how many pieces of fish was worth a piece of house furniture like a table or chair. These and so many other factors led to the introduction of currency.

However, the introduction of currency only motivated the people to work harder on their crafts and skills. Some expanded their ventures by acquiring more farmlands and more working tools to increase their productivity. Some others ventured into diverse skills and therefore started earning more currency than others.

As a budding or aspiring entrepreneur, your focus should not be on the currency but on the value you bring, the quality of service you render, and the problem you are able to solve.

Because sometimes, the value of a currency is limited by the environment and certain economic policies. It is the duplicity of quality service and innovations that inevitably attracts money and builds wealth.

The lesson to draw from the barter system is that everybody, no matter who they are, has something of value they can bring to the market place.
Just like I asked in the beginning of this section, what is your selling point?

If you were seated in a room with billionaires like Bill Gates, Jeff Bezos, Richard Branson, Warren Buffett, and others like them, with the barter lesson in mind, what would be that thing you possess that would be of interest to any of them?

What is that product or service you would sell them in exchange for their money, influence, or expertise?

If you can come up with a clear, straightforward answer, that right there is your selling point, which you ought to develop into a business.

However, if you cannot come up with a clear concept or idea of a selling point, it means you are not a problem solver yet.

Don't be dismayed if you are still trying to discover your selling point. The good news is that everyone has something of great value that God put inside of him or her with which they can live a purposeful life.

The fact that you haven't discovered it yet doesn't mean it's not there.

You probably have felt the inclination toward it in the past especially as a kid, but you were just too distracted to pay any conscious attention to it.

You just need to pay more attention to what your interests are by looking inward to discover it.

The Economics Of Emotional Intelligence

To be an effective problem solver, you have to understand the economics of emotional intelligence.

Emotional intelligence is the ability to understand how people think and behave. Because an understanding of how people think makes it easy to predict their behavior, you are easily able to identify and analyze their human nature, their basic needs, their wants and the means of solving them.

If you look around you, you'll see the different kinds of problems people face every day that need to be solved.

A thorough understanding of human behavior will give you a clearer picture on how to identify these problems and come up with creative ways to solving them depending on what capacity or skill set you possess.

The more creative you are with your product or service delivery, the more patrons you are likely to have.

Here are some of the human needs and wants that create problems just waiting to be solved.

1. *The need of people's inability to do things themselves***:** A lot of people are either too lazy or too busy to do things themselves. This is why they will always choose to leverage their time by paying someone else to do something for them, especially if it's a task that must be carried out. You can readily offer to get the task done and have them pay you for it.

For example, you can offer to take their kids to school, mow their lawns, shovel snow, prune their flowers, do their laundry, cook their food, and get paid for it.
This is why we have restaurants, gardening, and cab and chauffeur services available.

2. *The need to be social and gregarious*: People love leisure, love to socialize, be entertained and enjoy the pleasurable things in life. They will gladly pay for things that can help them laugh, relax, create fun and feel better about themselves.

If you are talented and can make people laugh, tell good stories, sing good songs and create pleasurable moments, you will get paid.

Comedy shows, blockbuster movies, top chart music videos, boat cruising, theme parks, amusement parks, and circus shows are some examples of things that create pleasurable moments in people's lives.

3. *The uncontrollable need to be successful:*
People are always looking for ways to improve their condition as it relates to their income, jobs, and positions.

They take up more hours in their jobs, take extra courses, acquire college degrees to improve on their skills, increase their earning power, and live a better, more fulfilled life. Even when they can't get it, they want it for their children. They want their kids to be in the best schools, stay ahead or at least on par with their peers.

Here you can offer training courses on business development, skill acquisition and tutorials on personal development to them or their children.

Examples are summer camps, seminars, business programs and other networking events.

4. *The need to be attractive to others:* People always think highly of themselves. A large majority want to be more beautiful, more intelligent, more sophisticated, and better looking than the next person and will gladly keep it so.

This is the reason you have increased demand for fashion and beauty products. People want to stay fashionable and beautiful to impress others, and there's nothing wrong with feeling so if you can afford it.

If you offer them unique beauty products, beauty enhancement procedures and services like makeup, plastic surgery, luxury items like designer brands, VIP and exclusive premium services they will pay you for it.

5. *The need to fill the void of ignorance:* The world is such a large place that nobody ever knows everything. Therefore, most of the decisions you make are made with an enormous amount of ignorance.

For example, you know very little about the structure and functionality of your anatomy, that's why you pay a doctor. You know very little about the dynamics of the laws governing your industry or the society you live in, that's why you pay a lawyer.

If you can leverage your wealth of knowledge in a particular field to provide vital information that solves problems and lifts people out of their ignorance you will get paid for it, especially if you can convert such knowledge into a smartphone app in this digital era. Mechanics, technicians, professors, lawyers, and doctors are some examples of professionals who can monetize their knowledge and expertise.

6. *The need to stay informed:* Quite similar to expertise monetization is information dissemination. People are ever searching for information that will improve their lives. They always want to keep ahead with the latest gossip and events happening around them and across the globe.

Provide them with up-to-date news as it unfolds, valuable tips on health or wealth creation. Give them exclusive interviews from known industry players or showcase the lifestyle of their favorite celebrities and you will get paid. Blogs, book publishing, cable news networks, radio stations, vlogs and podcasts are some examples of information dissemination channels.

7. The need for faster/quicker results: When it comes to getting things done, people are very impatient. People don't want to wait in line, they want to be served immediately. They want things done on the spot, especially in this "microwave" generation where nobody has the patience for process.

If you offer them a chance to get something done faster, they will gladly pay you for it. They want fast money and faster service.

For instance, if you asked them to choose between receiving something of value today or next week, of course they would tell you they want it today if it can be done.

An example is Amazon Prime and other express delivery services, the lottery, casino gambling and Ponzi schemes.

8. The need to be selfish and protective: The survival of the individual often depends on the individual's capacity to protect his or her interest first. The average human is always thinking about and looking out for themselves. They are always in the practice of advancing or protecting their own means before anyone else's.

Being selfish in this context is not a bad trait, as long as you don't cause harm to others in your venture. On a flight, you hear the flight attendant announce that you secure your oxygen mask first before trying to help another.

You can offer security, nutrition, immunity from harm, or a priority service to a self-seeking individual and they will gladly pay for it. Examples are security services, home security devices like door and window alarms, immunity from disease with vaccinations, protective gear during a pandemic, and so forth.

9. *The need for more value*: More money, more value, and more of everything especially good things. It is simply human nature to always prefer more to less because more is simply better than less. People want to be sure they are getting the best deals in all their transactions.

For this reason, they will do whatever they can to have more of the good things of life or get more value from doing business with others.

Nobody would take a job that pays less if they were offered the same job in the same field for more money, or ignore a service or product that offers more value over another.

You can become a middleman or broker who helps people acquire more value for a fee. Real estate agents, job websites, air ticket reservations, hotel reservations, healthcare and insurance service providers are all examples of brokers helping people to get more value.

How To Be An Effective Problem Solver

1. Observe And identify problems

With these traits that best describe how people are, it is up to you to identify your area of expertise and fill in the gaps.

To be an effective problem solver, you have to develop a high sense of curiosity, be readily observant and quick to identify these prevalent problems or needs.
These needs present the perfect opportunity for business ventures and ideas. I discuss this more in chapter 5.

2. Acquire and develop relevant skills

Now that you have identified the problems and needs, the next smart thing to do is to go acquire the relevant skills necessary for solving them.

Depending on the nature of the problem, ask yourself important questions such as is the problem solvable? If yes, does it require a new product or service or does an existing product or service need to be improved on?

The right answer to these questions will guide you on whatever step you need to take to bring about the required solution, be it product or service.

It is also important to note that you don't have to have a college degree to be a problem solver. However, if you must go to college, ensure that whatever discipline or course you choose to pursue is inspired by a major problem you wish to solve in society and not by a third party or peer pressure.

Most businesses you see around were inspired and birthed through this process of identifying and solving a societal problem.

3. Put your creativity to work

Creativity is the use of ideas, imagination, or experience to create something or improve on an already made product, idea, or invention. Being creative does not only help you create better solutions, it creates a positive experience that helps speed up the adoption of more ideas as time goes on.

We all have the potential to be creative, both as individuals and as team players. Creativity usually comes from the accumulation of knowledge gained from the books you have read, relevant stories you have heard, experiences acquired from trainings, consistent practice, and social interactions all stored up in the mind.

The more expanded your knowledge and experiences are, the more creative you will become. This is so because you are able to pull from a broader pool of know-how and experiences to make more meaningful connections that ultimately lead to new types of solutions.

I like to compare a creative mind to a kitchen cabinet filled with groceries and food condiment of all kinds. When hungry, as a good chef, it is very easy to reach into the cabinet and pull out whatever combination of food you desire to make.

You just select the right grain or pasta, choose your condiments, mix and apply appropriately, cook for a while and voila, your food is ready.

The same is not so for a mind devoid of knowledge and experience. No matter how good a chef (smart or intelligent) you may consider yourself to be, if your kitchen cabinet is empty, there will be nothing to cook or spice up your food.

If you are not constantly looking to improve your creativity by reading books and practicing new ideas, you may not be able to properly proffer solutions to problems as accurately and relevantly as needed and you could be stuck in a spot for a long time to come.

4. Apply the 80/20 and the 100-hour rule

The 80/20 rule, also popularly known as the Pareto principle, states that in many situations, roughly 80 percent of effects come from 20 percent of the cause. What that means in this context is that in your pursuit of success, 80 percent of your results will come from only 20 percent of your life's activities.

It is solely up to you to identify what these 20 percent activities are and then apply the 100-hour rule.

The 100-hour rule is basically centered on a simple question, which is, "If you had 100 hours to invest time, energy, and money into three ventures, what would it be?
What you are good at, what you are average at, or what you are bad at?

This question requires a moment of deep introspection before answering. Judging from many people's lives today, they seem to spread it equally, that is 33.3 percent across all three ventures. They want to be involved in anything and everything.

Smart and successful people do not think like that, they would consider it wise to do 95 percent, 5 percent, 0 percent or a 100 percent, 0 percent, 0 percent.

These two principles will help you streamline your thoughts and focus energy on what is most important and profitable, with proper clarity on what you ought to make your priority as a problem solver. So, forget about your weakness and focus on your strengths.

Focusing on your strengths as a problem solver makes it easy to identify problems that resonate with your skills or expertise thereby helping you produce faster and better results.

Therefore, invest most of, if not all, your effort in the things you are exceptionally good at.

5. Learn And practice

It is important that you give yourself to continuous learning and practice because there's usually the initial tendency to want to quit at the beginning especially when things don't go the way you planned or you discover it is more difficult than you had anticipated.

Just like it is with learning and practicing how to play music instruments such as the guitar or the piano, making money can be learned and practiced the same way.

By learning and practicing here, we mean that after acquiring knowledge in the form of a new skill or trade, you can start building little, focused steps aimed at making sound decisions with your income and capital and then following through with proper execution.

A continuous focus on learning and practicing will keep you afloat from quitting and we know that the more you learn the more you earn.

6. Take bold action and implement

Having identified the problem and acquired necessary skills to solving it, the next most important thing to do is to act accordingly by taking your idea to the marketplace and the public.

Because people are almost always initially wary or skeptical about new ideas and new ways of doing things, you'll have to be bold enough to defend and believe in your ideas, and also take the initial criticisms that might come your way in the early stage of your launch.

If your idea or solution is criticized, don't be discouraged but take it constructively.
Go back, learn some more, make amendments, improve on it, and present it again.
Sometimes, it takes multiple attempts to come up with winning ideas.

7. More problems, more money

Wealth creation has a formula, a formula almost as certain as a mathematical formula. This formula universally produces the same result anytime, anywhere.

It is very important to keep in mind that not every business venture will create wealth for you.

For your business to generate profit enough to get you out of poverty, it has to be easily scalable and essential in value.

This formula is all about making an effective impact. It states that the more lives you affect through a value you create, the richer you'll become. Simply put, the more people you can affect in the millions, the more money you will make.

To have it work for you, you need to ask yourself questions like, "How many lives can I touch?" "Who will benefit from my work?" "What value will my service or product add to society?"

For example, a sales person at a local retail store can only serve a few people in that locality and their income will only represent that same value. Compare that to a person who decides to create a mobile phone application that can be downloaded by millions of people from far and near.

The amount of money you have or don't have is a direct representation of the quality or quantity of value you have brought forth or not.

Action Steps

1. To be successful, you have to make yourself a person of value by becoming a problem solver.

2. To be a problem solver, there has to be some form of service or product you are selling in exchange for money.

3. By understanding how people are, what their needs and wants are, you are able to identify what problem they need solved.

4. After you identify the problems and needs, the next smart thing to do is to go acquire the relevant skills necessary for solving them.

CHAPTER
4

EDUCATION

Whenever the word "education" is mentioned, to a lot of people what comes to mind is a classroom, a school, or a completely formal setting where lectures are delivered while the students take notes. Others assume you are referring to some expensive MBA from a fancy school.

Gone are those days. The narratives have changed. Real education has shifted from the classroom to the practical world of work, skill, and solution providing – from general studies to specialized knowledge.

So when I say education, I'm not talking about schooling. I mean knowledge acquisition, not some crammed syllabus texts or curriculum to be regurgitated in the exam hall and forgotten ever after.

When it comes to knowledge acquisition, there is a big difference between schooling and learning.

Knowledge acquisition comes from learning not schooling. Schooling ends after graduation but learning is a continuous process.

To quit learning after graduation is a sure path down the road to poverty because what you learned in school is not enough to sustain you for the rest of your active life, especially considering the spate of inventions and innovations taking place every day.

You need to be in the habit of constantly reinventing yourself through knowledge acquisition especially the right kind of knowledge.

This kind of education is a vital ingredient in your quest for success. When you continually inject yourself with new skills, new competences, and new expertise, new roads of opportunities open up to you exposing you to higher chances of becoming very wealthy.

I'm not in any way trying to knock down the place of a college education, but the truth is that there's a shift happening in the corporate world today and it is ever so rapid.

Internet technology is rendering a lot of college expertise obsolete. Big corporations, for example, are fast ditching college grads to go for real-time solution providers in the persons of information technology and sales experts. Therefore, you cannot afford to stay mentally stagnant.

This is very evident in the top most successful enterprises and franchises today. You will notice that the majority of their staff do not possess college degrees.

Knowledge Is Prevalently Available

As it is today, you possess the innate ability to become an expert in anything that does not require physical talent. Why? Because knowledge has become prevalent.

In the history of mankind and civilization, I believe that this is the best time to be alive, simply because access to valuable information that makes us better people is a lot easier and most interestingly FREE.

It is a good thing you were not born in the fifteenth, sixteenth, or eighteenth century. We are certainly living in a time where the world is closing in on the wide gap between the rich and poor.

As it stands today, information has been democratized. Both the rich and poor now have access to the same kind of information. There's almost equal opportunity for anyone who is determined to make it, as long as you are willing to bring some value to the table.

Gone are the days when the common excuse for poverty was "because I couldn't afford a college degree."

If you are willing to drop your excuses, get to work, be prepared to put in the time and sweat required for the hustle, there's no limit to what you can achieve with an education.

Acquire and Apply Knowledge

Never has there been so much availability of resources and information to anyone who requires them. The question is, are you willing to drop your excuses, put in the work and learn?

The information is out there and most of it is free. There is so much you can learn and develop yourself with once you make up your mind to get into the habit of self-education.

More importantly, it doesn't matter how much information you possess, how many seminars you have attended, how many resources you have consumed or have access to, what is important is putting to practice what you have learned.

You have to be willing to put into practice what you have learned. This process is called self-education. If that is your desire, then here is how you can make the world around you a learning center, acquire more knowledge, and unleash your creativity.

How To Educate Yourself

1. *Develop a ferocious appetite for books*

What a map is to a treasure hunter is what a good book is to anyone looking to live a better life and improve him or herself financially, mentally, emotionally, physically, or spiritually. This fact can never be over emphasized; it is quite unfortunate that till this day and age, some people still underestimate the power of books.

Whether you believe it or not, all of life's secrets and formulas are contained in books. The reason you are still broke, depressed, or lonely is because you neglect and underestimate the power of reading.

When I say books, I'm not talking about some random romance or thriller novels. I mean business books, leadership books, biographies and autobiographies of great men and women who have already achieved what you are looking to achieve and living the life you wish to live.

I never knew this fact for sure until I started reading business and leadership books myself. My life literally took a dramatic turn around.

Books open up the eyes of your mind and give you a broader view of life from a very vantage perspective. If you are really serious about knowledge acquisition, the number of books in your library ought to at least be the same number as your age.

You have to deliberately cultivate the habit of relentless reading, a commitment to learning no matter your age or position in life. Invest in books that inspire, motivate, and challenge you to action.

It would shock you to know that most of the billionaires you have heard of started off as readers and are still readers till this day. If a billionaire like Warren Buffet and other rich guys with their busy schedules still find time to read, I wonder what your excuse is?

You might say you don't have time to read or don't know where or how to find the right material.

Bookstores and libraries are good places to start because no one will drop knowledge in your lap just like that, you have to go out and seek it.

Here is how you can convert some of your daily activities into classroom moments for learning.

Commuting class: If you drive, take an airplane, bus, train or cab, you can use that time to read a chapter or two depending on the duration of the journey. Instead of listening to music or tuning the stereo looking for the next hot gossip or depressing news, learn!

The toilet class: I know it sounds funny, but the truth is that you can also read a good book while you do your thing. That 10 or 20 minutes could change your life forever.

Waiting appointment class: When next you go for that doctor's appointment or any other visitation with an anticipated long wait, don't forget to take a good book with you, especially if it's going to be a long wait.

Gym/workout class: Among the places you can acquire knowledge, the gym is not left out. While you do your run on the street or treadmill, you can still imbibe knowledge in between your routines.

It's even become easier these days because you have books recorded on CDs, DVDs, MP3s and other audio materials that you can now listen to on the go by having someone else read them to you.

Some psychologists and educators believe that you only need to read three books on almost any field to have the basic practical knowledge of its applications.

2. *Get practical (the 40-hour principle)*

After books, the next best thing is getting practical. It takes 40 hours of dedicated practice time to become an expert in any of your area of interest. Yes, 40 hours, which is about an hour of practice every day for about a month and a half.

It could be less for some others but the generally applicable rule is 40 hours. You can teach yourself to become a writer, a web programmer, stock broking, sales, marketing, public speaking, fashion, a new language, and so much more if you are committed to it.

Just pick a field of interest and start learning. Again, you can teach yourself to become an expert in any skill you desire. You just have not bothered to find out how and there is no excuse not to.

Some of the computer apps you use today were not designed by computer scientists, a whole bunch of them were discovered by self-taught programmers who so desperately wanted to learn how to program. They read books on programming, scouted the Internet and spent hours practicing.

You learn from constant engagement, by getting out and taking action.

3. *Find mentors*

Having identified your area of interest you wish to develop yourself in, the next thing to do is to find experts in that field to mentor you.

You can do that by identifying very successful people in your area of interest: people whose lives are exemplary and worthy of followership and then study their lives with the hopes of understanding what they do differently.

Study how they behave, how they carry themselves, what their interests are, what their decision-making processes and daily habits are.

If you are going to make a trip to an exotic island or some distant location you've never been to before, I believe it is wise to inquire from people who have been there before. By doing so, you are creating a very sure, interesting path for your journey to success because you are following in the footsteps of those who have gone before you.

4. *Network more effectively*

Networking is the act of interacting, exchanging, and imbibing ideas or knowledge among people with a common profession and or special interest, usually taking place in an informal setting.

Networking as a tool for learning and upgrading your skills can happen between equals, colleagues, peer groups and age grades, and of course between the successful and the not successful or the aspiring to be successful, which is the sole purpose of this book and this chapter precisely.

It is amazing how people who aspire to be rich and successful only hang out and take advice from people of equal financial capacity and mental status with them or worse still, even lower.

This kind of association is very wrong. I'm not saying that you cannot have friends among your peers or colleagues of the same level, of course you can, but you just need to keep in mind that by being around and taking advice from people doing as fairly well as you are or even more broke than you are, you are simply placing a limit on yourself and blocking out your chances of acquiring new ideas and knowledge that can break you out of poverty.

If you want to be knowledgeably successful in any area of your life, you must seek out people who have gone ahead of you, have already done what you are looking to do successfully and learn from them.

If it means taking a long trip or paying a fee to get in their face, do it.

To become an effective networker, here are 5 steps to network the proper way:

Hang out more with successful people.
Be genuinely interested in them.
Ask intelligently relevant questions.
Be willing to help or offer value.
Tell compelling stories.
Upgrade Your looks.

5. *The Internet*

The Internet has an array of infinite knowledge at your disposal, most of which is free. The biggest universities on earth today are YouTube and Google.

These two platforms can give you endless access to websites, webinars, blogs, vlogs, and podcasts with real, life-changing information all at your fingertips, yet most people still ignore them and use lack of time as an excuse.

You can subscribe to business forums, sign up for newsletters and webinars from your chosen mentors to keep up and stay updated with the latest information about your industry or area of interest.

If you are really serious about self-education, then you need to cut down TV time and other time-consuming frivolities and learn. I discuss more on time management in chapter seven of this book.

6. *Expose yourself to learning environments*

Seminars and conferences organized by trusted entities are a good place to acquire knowledge. They add great value to you because they are usually an opportunity to mingle and network with a congregation of like-minded individuals.

Action Steps

1. Develop a ferocious appetite for books.

2. Convert some of your daily activities into classroom moments for learning.

3. Practice the 40-hour principle.

4. Expose yourself to learning environments.

CHAPTER
5

STARTING SMALL

A family friend told me of what happened to him many years back. He said that sometime around the late '80s, a friend of his tried to introduce him to real estate in Lagos, Nigeria.

According to him, the said friend had approached him one day to tell him about an opportunity to acquire and resell cheap plots of land in a certain remote area of Lagos.

He said the friend took him to the site and it happened that the area was an ancestral land owned and controlled by a large family group. They had just shared the properties and everyone was eager to sell their portion and move on to go do something else with the proceeds.

The friend noticing the disinterest on his face tried harder to convince him to purchase at least one plot with a promise to hook him up with a great bargain price using his influence as an indigene of the area.

The long and short of the story is that the man left that area without negotiating a single deal, not because he couldn't afford to, but his excuse? He had a good job with a good pay and so he didn't think it would make sense to invest his money on a property with such little or no value at all.

"No one in his right sense would waste money on such venture" he said. Well, fast forward, 10 to 12 years later, that area became what is known as Lekki Phase 1 today.

The area became one of the top 5 most expensive areas in terms of property value in Nigeria. The man has never stopped talking about that incident till this day.

And guess what? He was laid off from his job a few years later because of some technological upgrade. He still regrets missing out on that wonderful deal.

Why Start a Business?

Now why did I share that story? In today's world, there's no longer a single track to financial security. As it used to be back in the day, people went to school, got a degree, found a job, and stayed in the same job till retirement.

These days, jobs and career tracks are no longer as secure as they used to be years ago.

The days of organizing retirement and send-off parties for employees of 30, 40, or 50 years are fast fading away.

This is because technology is fast disrupting the corporate workspace. Manual activities are being replaced with automated systems: robots are replacing humans in the manufacturing sector; software applications are replacing secretarial and administrative duties.

So, even if you are gainfully employed at the moment with some form of pension or 401(k) saved up somewhere, chances are that you are not guaranteed your job till retirement.

Even if you barely make it to retirement, you are likely to outlive your savings because of increased life expectancy or increased dependence from friends and family.

If you are within the age range of 21 to 40 years old at the time of reading this book, there's a high chance you will live to be around 80 to 85 years old.

Do you honestly think that the meager earnings from your 401(k) savings will last you that long?

Another good reason why you should have a business or side income source is that if you are going to be wealthy, you cannot depend on just one source of income, especially one in which you have no direct control or cannot take advantage of limited time or build a system to advance output.

In this chapter we are going to explore what qualifies to be called a business, and how to develop a business mindset. I will outline and explain the various popular business models, analyze why businesses fail, and explore the right and wrong reasons for starting a business.

We will also demystify some of the excuses and false perceptions people have about starting a business and correct the lies about money that delay or deter people from starting a side income business.

Everyone who became a billionaire didn't get there through one source of income.
They created multiple business systems that generated money for them even while they slept, and they were able to do it because they chose to adopt the creator mentality over a consumer mentality.

The Creator Mentality vs the Consumer Mentality

One major attribute of a good businessman or businesswoman is the ability to demonstrate and establish a creator mindset over a consumer one.

Look at it this way, ever since you were born, your mind has been subjected to a life of consumption.

What I mean by that is that all your life, you've been conditioned to want products, buy products, and more importantly seek out the cheaper products in the form of bargains, discounts, and deals.

While a vast majority of the world's population fall into this category of consumers, you as a business-minded person should rather opt to be a producer or creator first before becoming a consumer. So instead of randomly buying products, why not sell products.

While others are rushing to fill up their buckets at the well, sell buckets. Instead of paying for basic services, learn to offer those services you pay others for.

The whole idea is to get you to break free from the consumption mentality and switch to a creator mindset.

It might not be easy at first, but once you adopt the creator mindset, you will notice that your mind and your line of thoughts begin to easily discern business opportunities and ideas as clearly as possible.

Business Models

In starting a business, it is important to understand, identify, and adapt a business model.

A business model can basically be said to be how a business owner hopes to make money. It describes how a company creates and delivers values.

Although there are several kinds of business models, an online research and consultant company recently narrowed them down to four main categories:

1 – Creator/Manufacturer: A creator acquires raw materials from suppliers and transforms them into finished products ready for consumers. For example, fashion designers, furniture makers, product inventors and innovators.

2 – Distributor/Retailer: A distributor or retailer buys an already-finished product from a manufacturer and resells the same product at a slightly higher price for profit. An example of a distributor or retailer is your local grocery store.

3 – Real Estate (Ownership/Management/Rental): In this category landed properties are acquired by long-term lease or outright purchase with the sole aim of renting out the space for a fee. Examples are car parks, event centers, sports arenas, and in some cases private airports.

4- Broker/Agent: A broker facilitates a transactional meeting between a buyer and a seller and receives a negotiated percentage as fee or commission for services rendered.

BUSINESS EXCUSES

It is important to keep in mind that certain business and personal excuses most likely arise from certain quarters, like friends, family, environment, and most dangerously yourself.

So, I feel the need to prepare your mind with some the excuses you are most likely to come up against once you decide to start your business.

I call them excuses because that is simply what they are and not who you are or what you represent.

1. *I Don't Know What Business To Do*

 This is a very common excuse a lot of people come up with when they are advised to start a business. They claim they don't know what to do, which is not true.

You very well know what to do, but the truth is that you are just scared that you might fail. If you took a moment to look around your environment this minute, I'm sure you'd come up with at least one solid idea of what business to do and make money.

One easy way to come up with business ideas is to focus on needs. Yes, other people's needs, wants, and solutions. All around you are people with needs waiting to be met. If you can help other people solve problems, you are already in business.

You do not have to look too far or think too deep. Just look around your immediate environment, your own life, your friends and family. Listen to the things they complain about, look at the products you use, is there something you don't like about them?

Think about the things you think are done wrongly or missing in a particular area of service. For example, is your service provider annoyingly incompetent?

Do you have a challenge finding the right color, right size, or the right price for an item? Is there a shop or item you like and wished was closer to you but the distance to the place is too far away, or maybe items you think ought to be in stock but are not?

If you answered yes, to some or all of these questions, well, there you have it, they are all problems waiting to be solved.

You can refer back to chapter 4 of this book to where I discussed the economics of human characteristics to help you identify a business you can operate.

2. Somebody Else Is Doing It

This excuse is easily the most common. I personally think it is laughable not to pursue a business idea because of this assumption.

I remember sharing a very brilliant business idea with a relative of mine sometime back. I broke down into bits all the vital aspects of the business, including the execution and marketing strategy.

She agreed that it was a good idea but that another company, a bigger brand, was already doing it. So what? I asked her. The long and short of the story is that she chickened out because of competition.

I'll tell you what, competition is very good for business and here's why I think so.
The fact that some other person is doing it is all the proof of concept you need.

That somebody else is doing it means that there's already an existing market for the product or service you intend to sell, therefore the time you would have expended educating or sensitizing customers on a new product is conserved.

Avoiding a business because of competition is like avoiding a particular dish because it has salt in it. Yes, competition in business is what salt is to food. The right sprinkle leaves the food tasting great and an excess of it will mess up the taste because of the law of demand and supply.

The truth is that there's hardly anything new in terms of products or service these days. Everything that is to be made has been made already. People just take an already existing product or service and improve on it, talk about creativity at work.

To get creative with an existing product or service, think of how you can educate people, make them feel better, or bring them pleasure in a different way.

3. I Don't Have Enough Money

This is another most common excuse a lot of people give as a reason for not owning a business or pursuing their passion.

Don't get carried away by the popular notion that you need money to make more money.

Money is very important, no doubt, but it is not the only thing you need to create a start-up or a business. You also need time, and time is in fact, more important than money.

You need to invest time by taking some moments to understudy what business venture to involve yourself in, or if you already have an exact idea of what business you want to engage in, start spending time with the people who are already in the business.

That way, you learn more about the nitty-gritty and intricate aspects of the business and also learn from their mistakes.

Another reason I believe time is more important than money is that no matter when you start, it usually takes an average of five to ten years to stumble through and build a business to stability. Therefore, the earlier you start, the sooner you get there.

I remember some years back, around 2012, and 2014, when I was job seeking in Nigeria. My father offered to give me a start-up loan to start a clothing business.

At that time, all my mind was engrossed with was finding the ever-evasive job that never came, I had actually scoffed at the idea of selling cloths and after several attempts at trying to convince me by my father, he simply let me be.

Fast forward several years later to 2018, I started reading and researching on how to start and grow a business, and when I decided to start my first business, guess what it was – your guess is as good as correct, the same clothing business I ignored back then.

Today, through trial and error, mistakes and corrections, I buy from a supplier and resell to my customers both online and offline. Despite the fact that the profit is good, I still can't stop imagining how much my business would have grown and what I would have learned by now if I had heeded to my father's advice to go learn the trade back then.

As I mentioned earlier, building a business takes time and so, the sooner you start the sooner you build and grow your business empire.

Instead of wasting your time on social media and watching movies with compelling stories that add no value to your life, why not devote or volunteer your free time toward learning about a business or a particular job you desire, pending when an opportunity will present itself.

Money in a new business ought to be like gasoline or a magnifying glass that makes your fire bigger, enables you move quicker and learn faster by granting you access to better resources, tools, and channels.

Don't be one of those waiting for the perfect time when an angel will show up out of nowhere and drop cash on them to go start up something.

This mentality is wrong and I say so because nobody who has worked hard for their money would just shell out money to an idle person.

Start something today no matter how small and grow from there.

4. I Don't Have The Time

We all have the same 24 hours in a day – every one of us, both the successful and the yet to be successful.

If you really think about it, nobody ever has the time. The difference is in how you manage your time.

If you are really serious about starting a business as a full-time job or as an alternative source of income, you will surely make the time, no matter how tight your schedule may seem.

You can actually start managing and using your time wisely by cutting off some the activities in your life that stealthily steal your time. Things like TV and social media (see chapter 7 of this book).

You can also find time by deciding to start your day earlier in the morning, say at about 5 a.m. That way you gain an extra hour or two to devote to your business.
Think about this for a moment, if millionaires and billionaires either go to bed or wake up at 5 a.m., why then should you, a work in progress be having 9–10 hours of sleep?

Procrastination

Procrastination is no doubt the biggest thief of time and dreams. The problem with people in this category is not the dearth of business ideas but the lack of will to actually start the business. They intentionally keep delaying and postponing the day of action for the flimsiest of reasons, such as the next point.

Pride

A combination of false pride and irrational ego can create in people a distorted and exaggerated image of their own importance. There are people who delude themselves into believing that certain business activities are "beneath them."

For this category of people, no matter how profitable a business venture or proposal you present to them might seem, they will never put in the work or get their hands dirty because they are always too shy or embarrassingly concerned about what others would think or say.

Sadly, what the people who fall into this category fail to realize is that the same people you are trying to impress with your false sense of conceit will be the first to mock you when they eventually discover your true state of insolvency.

There are lots of business ventures that might require you to get off your high horse and get dirty but surely promise great returns in income and profit.

There's also the pride of self-doubt, which has to do with the fear of suffering the indignity of failure should the business fail in the long run.

Too Risky

According to Jim Rohn, "People would do better, if they knew better." By these words, he was referring to the large percentage of people who would rather stick to a job they hate for 40 years, get drunk on weekends, detest Mondays, speak evil about their boss behind their back and still suck up to them at the same time.

They hate their life, feel miserable, depressed and yet never explore their potential because of the fear of losing money if the business goes wrong.

My question to you is would you rather fail and learn from the experience, or not try at all and live with regret for the rest of your life.

The thing about failure is that the pain of the loss is only for a while. You take consolation from the fact that you at least gave it a shot and learned from the experience, just like Thomas Edison said after several failed attempts at inventing the light bulb.

Somebody had asked him when he was going to stop wasting his time after several failed attempts at getting the bulb to work. He simply replied by saying, "Well, at least I now know several ways not to do it."

When you try and don't succeed, you learn how not to do it and seek to become better. But when you don't try at all because you fear the risk of losing money and chose to play it safe by not taking action, the regret is forever. Especially when you see the positive results of the people who were willing to take the risk at the time.

Again, I ask you, would you rather take the risk and fail, than not try at all and live with the regret for the rest of your life? The choice is yours.

Power Points

1. There's no longer a single track to financial security because of disruptions caused by the continuous developments in technology.

2. Develop and establish a creator mindset over a consumer one.

3. It is important to keep in mind that the moment you decide to start a business, certain personal excuses will most likely arise from certain quarters, like friends, family, environment and most dangerously yourself.

4. It is better to take the risk and fail, than not try at all and live with the regret for the rest of your life.

CHAPTER 6

MARKETING AND EXECUTION

Once you've made up your mind on a choice of business, your next line of thought should be on execution. By execution, I mean a functional marketing strategy.

For any business venture to be successful, whether it is self-owned or you are working for somebody, there has to be a clear-cut, well-executed marketing plan.

A marketing plan is an operational strategy on how a business or organization intends to advertise and present its products and services to its target audience.

No matter how excellent or efficient a business is, if it not well marketed, it will fail. Suffice to say that there are lots of good products, brands, and services that exist out there in the market but poor execution and marketing has kept them in obscurity.

Almost everything you've paid for was marketed to you in one form or another.
You probably saw a TV ad, a center spread ad in a magazine, a billboard, a radio jingle, Internet pop up or somebody told you about it through word of mouth. One way or another, you were exposed to a product or service through marketing before you came to know about it.

Therefore, marketing is a very crucial factor to consider when starting a business.

It is important to know that there is a huge difference between marketing and selling. A lot of business owners and service providers mistake selling for marketing, causing them to focus and dissipate resources on the wrong things.

When you are selling, you are only focused on the functionality of the product or service you are rendering. Your goal is to close a deal at all costs, even if means making bogus and unrealistic claims about your product or service.

An effective marketing message is not a competition or a race to the finish line. It is an act of service that anchors on solving the prospective customers' problems and providing solutions, taking into consideration their emotional needs, expectations, and reactions.

For example, "I can sell ice to an Eskimo, I can sell water to a well, or
I can sell sand to a desert,"... are all examples of skillful selling not marketing.

The above examples of skillful selling are the reason a lot of people dread and avoid salespersons because they can be very smooth and persuasive individuals who just won't take no for an answer, consequently, making you pay for what you don't need.

However, an effective marketing plan takes into consideration a target audience, their specific age range, gender, their thoughts, behavior, needs, and personality.

Quite similar to emotional intelligence, this knowledge easily helps you predict your prospective customers' fears, frustrations, and other forms of emotions that compel people to use your service.

To craft a great marketing plan, it is crucial to properly research only the opinions of your prospective customers because no other opinion matters except theirs, not even your own opinion as the producer.

This is why proper research of your target audience is vital. Your findings will help tailor your message specifically for them, especially regarding the use of certain keywords that excite their emotions.

How To Craft A Great Marketing Campaign For Your Brand

Just like strings on a guitar, human emotions can be played the same way. Knowing the right chords to play makes good music, but a careless tug at the strings of a guitar is nothing but noise to the ears.

The right keywords in your marketing message will trigger an emotional response from your prospective customers. A good marketer knows that it is better to appeal to people's emotions than their sense of logic.

This is because people tend to react faster emotionally than they do logically.

Some examples of these catchy keywords and phrases are free, cheaper, better, bigger, extra, great deal, discount, safer, healthier, easier, longer lasting, discover new ways, your comfort, save more money, helping you, and so on.

These words can be classified into five basic emotions and they are *fear*, *ego*, *guilt*, *sense of affection*, and *greed*.

If you pay close attention, you'll notice that some of the best ad campaigns on TV, radio, news magazines and social media always contain one or more of these emotional strings.

I'm going to demonstrate to you how they subtly input them in their messages so you too can do the same with your brand.

I call them the FEGGS of marketing and they are as follows:

i. Fear: if you are trying to sell padlocks, for example, you'll get more attention if your ad is able to show the dangers and risks of home burglary and break-ins than it would over emphasizing on the quality or the engineering expertise in the production of the padlock.

The fear of having their home burgled will definitely prompt a reaction because people will more likely pay to avoid a loss than they will to gain something.

ii. Ego: Deep down within us, we all have our ego, and our ego loves to win. Whenever you hear or see phrases like "make them green with envy" or "for a smoother, softer, glowing skin," you already know the message is pulling on your pride. The use of comparatives like smoother, bigger, or better is aimed at eliciting some form of subtle competition.

iii. Guilt: This type of marketing appeals to your sense of guilt and conscience. It makes you feel bad for not fulfilling the purchase.

iv. Greed: Sometimes the word "greed" does not connote negativity, especially in this circumstance. As humans, there's always a natural tendency to want more of good things, especially for less price or even free of charge. For example, "buy one, get one free," "50 percent discount," or "same value, lower price" are all marketing examples of providing more for less.

v. Sense of Affection: "The perfect gift for her this Valentine's Day," or "Reignite your love" are both examples of marketing messages that target your sense of affection for a loved one.

These emotional strings should be best applied at the introductory part of your marketing message. This is because you want your message to attract and sustain your targeted customers' attention from the beginning to the end.

However, these emotional hot buttons as powerful as they are, when they are too obvious or overused can have the reverse effect.

So make sure to be very subtle and have the best interest of your customers when applying any of them.

Power Points

1. There is a huge difference between marketing and selling.

2. People react faster emotionally than they do logically.

3. Almost everything you've paid for was marketed to you in one form or another.

Action Steps

1. When crafting a marketing message, always research your target audience.

2. Be sure to be subtle when applying the FEGGS keywords in your marketing campaign.

CHAPTER 7

TIME, YOUR MOST UNDERRATED ASSET

Recently, I was running an errand in town and somehow I ended up in a hospice for elderly people. I spent quite some time there and seeing these lovely old men and women in their different states of frailty, the true meaning of that popular quote suddenly began to make sense to me: "Make hay while the sun shines."

As a kid, I always heard this quote but never really gave it deep thought or even sought to understand how that applied to me.

For a moment, it got me thinking about my own life and life in general. The proverb simply means that you take advantage of the chance to do something while the conditions are good.

In agriculture, hay is mown grass that has been cut and dried in the sun to be used as food for cattle. The sun as we know shines brightest in the middle of the day. Therefore, the idea of making hay while the sun shines is a perfect representation of the days of our lives here on earth.

The days of our lives on earth are numbered. Whatever you are today, is what you created yourself with your time and what you will become tomorrow depends on how you use your time today.

Time as a Measurement of Life

Life is like a normal 24-hour day. Just as there is the morning, the noon, evening, and late night in a day, so it is with life.

Between the ages 0–18 years, is the morning time of life, ages 19–49 years are the noon time, ages 50–65 years are the evening time of your life, and ages 66 and beyond are the late night.

Every one of us falls in one of these age brackets, it is therefore very pertinent that you make the best of the time you have when the conditions are right and favorable to avoid carrying over the burdens of one phase into the next.

There is a time for everything. From the time you were born to the time you die, it is expected that certain activities and experiences ought to have been accomplished.
That way, you easily move on to the next phase of your living and learning experience.

Time as a Form of Currency

Time like currency must be spent. Therefore, you are either investing time or squandering it.

Rich or poor, black or white, old or young, everyone is allotted the same amount of time, 24 hours every day.

Just like you spend money to buy things, what do you spend your time on? Who do you spend your time with?

Any time spent doing things that do not bring financial increase, mental development, spiritual or physical wellness is wasted time. Such time squandered in frivolity can never be recovered or accounted for.

For some people, time is more valuable and important than money. They'd rather pay more to get something done faster than waste long hours haggling or scouting the market for days looking for cheaper prices.

So what you do while the clock ticks away each second matters a lot. Make your time worthwhile by investing it in activities that bring you value.

Time Never Stops

Time is very precious and waits for nobody. Time cannot be stopped. It is impossible to pause an hour in the day; however, you can control and manage it.

Take a look at your watch and the calendar right now, whatever time and date you see will pass and never be seen again.

Regardless of what time of the day it is right now, as soon as the clock strikes 12 midnight today, it already becomes a new day and yesterday will have gone forever, never to be seen again.

Time is a Rewarder

Your existence on earth can be likened to that of a hired laborer on the clock: a worker hired to accomplish a specific task for which at the end of the working day, you are rewarded by the supervisor with wages for a job well done or receive nothing for doing nothing.

Time rewards every one according to how well they have utilized it. If you sit around idly and choose to do nothing, time will pay you accordingly. However, if you utilize your time being productive, time will reward you with the results you seek.

Time-Wasting Habits

Habits as we know are difficult to get rid of and time-wasting activities are like habits.

These habits have become so ingrained in your daily routines that you spontaneously indulge in them without even thinking. They surreptitiously steal your time and waste your productive years.

If you are able to identify, avoid, or replace some of these time-wasting activities with productiveness, I guarantee you that your life in 5 or 10 years' time will be 40 percent better than those who cluelessly continue to indulge in them.

Here is a list of some of those time habits that gradually steal your life away without you knowing.

1. TV and movies

Research has shown that the average human watch about 5 hours of television a day.

This translates to about 35 hours a week. Multiply 35 hours by 52 weeks (a year) that gives you 1,820 hours. Divide that by 24 hours (a day), what you get is a whopping 75 days – approximately two and a half months of just TV time in a year and you still wonder why you are broke?

This is just on TV, by the time we are done with our analysis, you can be the judge of your own life.

2. Browsing social media

The amount of media content consumed on the platforms of Facebook, Instagram, and other interactive apps is overwhelming to say the least.

These days it is not unusual to see couples at tables on a date with eyes seriously glued to their phones; same with people on the streets, at the mall, on the bus, on the train, and just about everywhere you go.

According to Business Insider, a leading online business blog, while TV viewing time may have decreased for some people, there has been a high spike and continuous increase in the amount of viewing time spent on streaming platforms such as Hulu and Netflix because of the originality of content that can only be streamed online.

This viewing and interactive convenience constitutes for an average smartphone user about 2 hours a day of browsing and scrolling through chatting apps and streaming platforms.

That is about 14 hours a week, 728 hours a year, divided by 24 hours is another 30 days spent on frivolous online entertainment.

Instead of surfing the Internet looking for the next piece of gossip or sensational news, why not use that time to listen to inspirational materials littered all over the net.

3.Oversleeping

Although sleep is undeniably an essential ingredient for human functionality, over indulging is sleep abuse.

The Bible in Proverbs chapter 6 verse 10 and 11 KJV version says, "Yet a little sleep, a little slumber, a little folding of the hands to sleep: So shall thy poverty come as one that travelleth, and thy want as an armed man."

There has always been controversy about the duration of sleep that a person requires. Some say 6 hours, some say 8, but I'd say from experience, 6 hours is enough time for any serious-minded person who really wants to be successful to catch all the rest they need.

If you are an 8- or 9-hour sleeper, at the end of a given year, put together, you would have slept for 4 months.

Sleep, is essential, but should be done in moderation.

4. Phone calls and chitchat

This habit is also a major time-waster. I'm sure reading this right now, you know someone who spends long hours on the phone during the day talking about nothing important but just gossip, even in the face of work piled up in front of them.

It is worse these days, with the introduction of WhatsApp and Facebook calls that make it way cheaper to make extended calls especially international without worrying about extra charges to phone bills.

Think about it this way, an average of about 40 minutes a day of phone conversations gives you 280 minutes a week, which translates to about 10 days of talking on the phone in a year.

With the exception of phone calls that are business-related or an emergency, you ought to learn how to round off calls in 5 minutes and focus on the day's tasks.

5. Commuting time

The average working adult spends upward of 25 to 30minutes in traffic to work and another 30 minutes back. This could be more, if you live in a heavy traffic area, but let's just use 30 minutes as the average time.

If you work Monday to Friday as it is with most people, it translates to about 5 hours a week and 10 days a year, spent on the road; remember it could be more depending on your location.

6. Procrastination

The real reason a lot of people are still living broke or stuck financially is not because they lack ideas. They are just not ready to take the bold step yet. They are waiting for the perfect time, which will never come.

You should bear in mind that there's no such thing as the perfect time or the perfect moment, you are the one to take the moment and make it perfect.

Year after year, months and days pass by, each time you come up with a convenient reason why you can't start that business, why you can't move out of your current location, or why you can't afford that life-transforming seminar at the moment.

What you don't know is that as you continue to do that, you are only postponing your next level.

That phone call, that book you ought to write, that movie you ought to produce, that business meeting or seminar you are procrastinating over could just be the stepping stone you need to journey into discovering your world of greatness. If you don't do it, it stays undone forever.

7. Waiting for a miracle

Albert Einstein said, "Don't wait for a miracle, your whole life is already a miracle."
A lot of people have wasted years of their lives praying, hoping and waiting on a miracle that will drop from the sky.

For some, 5 out of the 7 days of the week, they are in church or at home fasting and praying with the hope that God would send help to their doorstep.

Don't get me wrong, I would never joke or underestimate the power of prayer. I pray, but what you don't know is that prayer is only a catalyst for activating the process of your success.

You ought to launch out after you have prayed and not go back to lie on your couch. The Bible in James chapter 2 verses 26 says, "Faith without work and corresponding action is a waste of time."

You don't need any other miracle other than the greatest miracle of having the breath of life in your nostrils.

The fact that you are born in this generation and this time is the greatest thing to ever happen to you. What if you were born in the fifteenth century or during World War I and II when the world didn't know much?

Reading this right now is also a miracle, so you don't have to wait any longer. It is time to go to work with your talents, your gifts, your passions and ideas because while you are waiting for God, God is waiting for you to take the first step.

8. Miscellaneous

Other time-wasters are video games, ailments, political and sports debates, and so on.

The Result

If you add the two and a half months of TV time, one month of social media, 10 days of phone conversations and 10 days of commuting to and from work alone, in a year you will have spent about 4 months out of 12 months on play and leisure.

If you add the four 4 months of sleep, though essential, that comes to about 8 months.

Over a 10-year period, you will have squandered seven and a half years of your life doing absolutely nothing beneficial, mentally or financially.

This is the reason you leave people and meet them again after many years and they are still the same, financially and mentally.

Instead of going to the game or movies, how about you become deliberate about your choice of company. Why not decide to start hanging out with business-savvy friends, family members, or even mentors so you can learn what they do and do the same or even do it better.

Instead of surfing Facebook and Instagram, why not do some research on businesses you can take on, and new skills or new international languages you can learn to make your brand a global one if you already have a business.

When I say research, I don't just mean asking Google a bunch of random questions; you need to invest time and money in business books and business magazines both online and offline.

You should never be too tired or too lazy to read books. The power of reading can never be underestimated.

Whatever you are today is what you bought and paid for with your time.

Power Points

1. The days of our lives on earth are numbered. Whatever you are today, is what you created yourself with your time and what you will become tomorrow depends on how you use your time today.

2. Rich or poor, black or white, old or young, everyone is allotted the same amount of time at their disposal, 24 hours every day.

3. Time-wasting activities are like habits – if you are able to avoid and replace some of these time-wasting activities with productiveness, your life in

5 or 10 years' time, at the barest minimum will be 30 to 40 percent better than it is today.

CHAPTER
8

SET CLEAR GOALS

Imagine a pilot getting in an airplane and taking off without a destination. No matter how impressive his flying skill is or how new the airplane engine maybe, if he continues to fly around without a destination, chances are that he will run out of gas one day and crash.

He can not be compared to the one who picks a location, determines the distance, considers the amount of time and fuel it would cost to arrive at his destination before setting out.

The difference between the two pilots is that the one with a location in mind will not only conserve fuel, energy and time. He is also able to keep track of his progress with a clear knowledge of distances covered and distances remaining.

I remember as kids when we used to play soccer in the parks and open fields. Usually, we would choose our teams of 4, 5, 6 or even 10 aside, depending on the size of the park and how many kids were available to play at the time.

Interestingly, whenever we first arrived in a group and approached the field, the person with the ball, out of excitement, would kick it high up in the air into the field and everybody would rush after the ball.

Whoever got to the ball first would just start dribbling it around. He did not pass to anybody, but was just running around and displaying skills with the ball until he was tackled by another person who did the same thing.

It continued like that for some minutes but after a while, the initial excitement faded. We all became bored and tired, then decided to set up a goal post and choose the members of our teams.

I had to reference this because this is the experience in the life of so many. Some people work so hard but without aim, purpose, or objectives.

A goal is the sole aim and objective of a person's ambition, the destination of a journey, and the end target of a project or activity.

It is an observable and measurable end result of set of objectives to be achieved within a given period of time.

Without goals, you will ignorantly run in circles and before you know it, wear yourself out in frustration.

A life of hustle without goals is boring and will cause you to tap out easily.

No matter how interesting you think your life is right now, if you don't set goals, it will soon become frustrating. To get ahead and stay ahead, you need to set goals for yourself.

Effective goal setting is a very crucial component for achieving success in any area of your life, whether career, relationship, finance, or family.

Setting goals induces your mind to see your future before it actually happens. It demystifies the whole idea of success as an evasive enigma. It also positions you closer and face to face with success waiting for you to grasp it.

Personally, setting goals really helped shape my life for good. All my life I'd always heard different people talk about goal setting and how important it is but I never really gave it any serious attention.

The most I did was just scribble a mental note in my head and that was it. Other times I would just write down some grandiose, unrealistic dreams without any clear-cut plan for how to achieve them. All of which I simply forgot after a while.

My moment of transformation started after I listened to some teachings on the subject of goals and goal setting. I learned that it is not enough to just think about it.

Your goals have to be specific, concise, realistic, measurable, and documented for easy mental assimilation. I took up the advice and decided to do just as the person said.

What then is goal setting you ask? Goal setting is the process of identifying and deciding what you want to accomplish and devising a clear, concrete plan toward achieving that desired result.

How To Set Goals

Since we already know that a goal is an observable and measurable end result of a set of objectives to be achieved within a given period of time, it is therefore important that we also expand on some of the characteristics of a goal.

1. Write it down: The first step and one of the most fundamental aspects of goal setting is to write the goal down. This is very important because research has shown that a goal written out makes the writer over 60 percent more likely to achieve it.

Writing your goals down improves your recall and recital of the vital information contained in it. It also helps your mind focus on more important stuff and the people relevant to your life.

2. *Read it every day:* After you have written it down, it is very important that you read your goal to yourself at least twice every day. In the morning when you wake up and at night before you go to sleep.

Frequent reading of your goals fires up your creativity and empowers you with unusual streaks of motivation and energy to want to do more and push yourself beyond your limits.

3. *Tell others:* This is optional, but by choosing to tell others or someone close, you are making them hold you accountable for the things you desire to accomplish within a given period of time.

By telling others you put yourself in the spotlight, and because you do not want to be seen as a failure or mere talker, you are birthing an extra reason why you not only must pursue your goals but also see that they are achieved.

4. *Be precise:* A precise goal is easier to achieve than an ambiguous one. For example, if you decide that you want to earn more money, it's not enough to just say "I want to earn more money." You have to specifically state how much and within what period of time.

By writing down something like "I want to earn an extra $2,000 on the side every month," you already know you are off to a good start.

The next thing to do is take it a step further by breaking the $2,000 down in to chunks, say about $70 a day. With such a precise breakdown, you make your goals clearer to understand, easier to visualize, and easier to achieve.

Writing your goals down and reciting them to yourself every day almost immediately makes you feel a certain switch in your mind and inundates you with an unusual rush of refreshing energy flow.

You begin to see your job and tasks differently. I'm not even talking about the sense of triumph and accomplishment you' feel every time you meet your daily or weekly set goal.

This puts a reason behind your aim, which will enable you push further even when it may become challenging.

5. *Track your progress:* When it comes to effective goal setting, tracking your progress is critical. Setting clear parameters will allow you to track your progress and know when you have achieved your goal.

For example, "save more money" is not a measurable goal, it's unclear what "more" means here. You need to have solid metrics in mind.

Observe your spending patterns, monitor where a large chunk of your money goes and determine if it is on needs or mere wants.

If it is on needs, not much of a problem but if they are just wants, then you should check your impulsive buying habits.

The same thing applies to your health and relationship. Always keep a measurable track of your exercise routines and activities. For example, it's not enough to just go out and run.

You need to set a timer to determine the duration and the distance covered per workout session. That way you strive to outdo your previous performance the day before.

6. *Make it attainable and realistic:* There's nothing wrong with setting very lofty goals for yourself, but the truth is that when you set such grandiose targets without any clear-cut strategy or mechanism in place to actually achieve them, it will frustrate you.

For example, you're not going to create a billion-dollar business or become a world-class concert pianist or sports celebrity overnight if you have never run a business or played an instrument before, ever.

It is better to break it down in to tiny chunks of daily and weekly activities and actions.

A gradual compounding of these actions over time evolve into a full-blown mastery in your field of endeavor. So, keep it simple, realistic, and within reach. You can always reset and adjust when you surpass each goal.

7. Have a deadline or timeline: Having a clear idea of your timeline creates a sense of urgency that pushes you to work toward what you want more quickly.

For example, if your goal is that you want to learn Spanish because it will help you communicate better with your clients from Spanish-speaking countries, what you do is set a realistic time frame for you – say, 6 months.

Setting a timeline for a goal such as this is just so that you can continually check in with yourself along the way because anything that takes longer than necessary can easily become overwhelming.

Try setting goals that can be realistically achieved within a 12-month period. Set yourself up for success by concentrating on what can be achieved in the short term. If you do have a long-term goal in mind, break it down into smaller goals that can be achieved in a year.

Types of goals

There are different categories of goals and they vary in priority according to your age and purpose.

Also, there are long-term and short-term goals.

While long-term goals involve the things you hope to get done in ten to twenty years' time, short-term goals are almost immediate and are broken down into steps of yearly, monthly, weekly, and daily activities for easy adherence and follow up.

These include but are not limited to:

1. Financial goals: Financial goals means different things to different people. It is the process of actively taking charge of your earnings, spending, and savings throughout your active work life to when you are retired.

It comprises of money you seek to earn, spend, and save on a daily, weekly, monthly, and yearly basis and over a fifteen to twenty year period of time. For most people, the biggest long-term goal for them is saving enough money to retire.

2. *Career goals:* A career goal is a well-defined statement explaining the profession you intend to pursue throughout your career. Whether you are an employee, a job seeker, a businessman, businesswoman, or entrepreneur, it is very important that you define your career goals clearly.

A clear career goal easily helps you adopt and implement effective action plans involving both the short term and long term. It should at least contain but not be limited these crucial aspects:

Upgrading your professional knowledge and training
Increased earnings
New experiences
Leadership role

3. *Family goals:* Family goals are family vision and mission statements by which a family abides.

Family goals are very important because they consist of a variety of resolutions with a single purpose or outcome in mind, which is to bring and keep the family closer through activities that foster love, harmony, and affection.

Action Steps

1. The first step and one of the most fundamental aspects of goal setting is to write your intention down.

2. Be precise and vocal about your goals.

3. Set a deadline.

CHAPTER 9

CREATE YOUR OWN LUCK WITH YOUR ACTIONS

The word luck means several things to different people.

To a flat broke person, luck is waking up every day and hoping that a miracle or good fortune will happen to him and change his life forever; while for a successful person, luck means creating your own fortune by basically preparing, packaging and positioning yourself for opportunities with a readiness to grab it whenever it shows up.

This is why it looks like some people are always "lucky" and some are not.

Seek Adventures and Venture Into the Unknown

I heard the story of a soldier captured behind enemy lines and detained as a prisoner of war.

One day the commander of his captors came to him and said, "Tomorrow you will be facing the firing squad, but you have a choice."

He pointed to a door not too far away from where the prisoner was being held and said to him, "You can choose to walk out that door or surely face the firing squad."

The prisoner, confused and curious at the same time asked his captor, "What is on the other side of that door?"

"I don't know, no man has ever agreed to walk through that door," the commander replied.

The prisoner said he'd rather face the firing squad than walk through into the unknown, so early the next morning, they took him out to the fields and executed him.

A few days later, one of the commander's subordinates out of curiosity asked his commander, "What is on the other side of that door?"

"Freedom," he replied.

I am a firm believer in the saying that it is better to try, and not make it, than not trying at all. This is because by not trying, you never know for sure what the outcome would have been.

It has been observed that some people prefer their known hell to an unknown heaven.

A lot of people want to be successful yet don't want to take any risk of trying something new. They are afraid to take bold steps, dump their old friends, or change location while pretending to be OK with their below-average life.

How do you expect to win a prize in a race you are not a participant in?

I like to tell people who are afraid of taking risks – whether in business, relationships, or work – that you can never learn how to swim without getting wet.
No matter how many theory lessons you acquire, there has to be the point where you get into the water, the shallow end of the water at least and start swimming.

The good thing about this swimming analogy is that as a beginner, no one expects too much from you, therefore you do not have to worry about making mistakes or starting slow.

There is such a thing as the law of cause and effect. This universal law of cause and effect states that for every effect there is a cause, likewise for every cause, there is an effect.

Your thoughts, behaviors, and actions create specific causes that create and drive your life in a certain way. It means that for every step you take in line with your dreams or plans, there's always an effect in the form of reward if successful or lesson learned if unsuccessful.

Interestingly, the same law applies when you have an idea or plan to be successful and choose to do nothing, doing nothing in itself is a cause and the resultant effect is nothing to show.

It is time to take action. Any knowledge acquired and not applied is useless knowledge. You have read enough books and attended enough seminars. It is time to launch out.

Never be Afraid to Seek Greener Pastures

Two frogs were put into a pot of water and the pot placed over a lit stove. Studies have revealed that frogs have a way of adjusting their body temperature to blend with their current environment.

As the temperature in the pot increased, the frogs started getting restless. The water got warmer and the two frogs kept adjusting their body temperatures. The warmer it got, the more restless they became.

At some point, one of the frogs couldn't take the heat anymore and jumped out.

The other frog stayed in and kept adjusting his body temperature to the now boiling water. A few minutes later, the frog reached his body temperature limit and died.

It is possible that you are in the category of people facing this in their lives at the moment. You have resided in a particular vicinity, neighborhood, state, or country for the most part of your life yet you've got nothing to show for it.

You are still broke, despite all your struggles and efforts to get better. Could it be that you are currently residing in a location or environment that is hampering and hindering your development?

Geographically or environmentally, the energy, traditions, and mentality of the people you surround yourself with on a daily basis have a way of affecting you, positively or negatively.

A Lamborghini no matter how clean and sleek it may look can never perform to its fullest capacity in a desert or mud bank.

Some seeds by nature cannot germinate in certain soil. It is the same with people who are in the wrong locations.

For example, if you were a female born in an overtly religious country like Iran, war-torn countries like Yemen and Syria or any other underdeveloped third-world country, chances are that you would be denied the right to basic education and probably be married off at a tender age of 13 or 14 and most likely never get the chance to pursue your personal dreams and ambitions.

Compare that to a child born in Australia or Switzerland who has access to basic education and whose fundamental rights to the pursuit of personal development is guaranteed.

I have met quite a number of individuals with great talent, skills, and personalities, many of who are unable to cultivate or harness their gifts beyond its crude stage.
Such people live and die with their gifts inside of them because they were born and by choice remained in a location lacking in social infrastructure and amenities required for human capacity development.

You may not have chosen your birthplace, but you have a choice about where you will end up.

If you live in a country where you have to struggle to access the basic social amenities necessary for human development like quality education, health care, funds for business startups, then it is time you started thinking about relocating.

You should move to a more developed country with greater advantages where you will have access to better tools and better resources without having to worry about basic needs.

The same thing applies to your environment. If you were born and bred in a state or neighborhood that consists of below-average individuals, chances are that you will never be inspired enough to aspire to be in the top echelons of society.

You must be willing to open yourself up to the possibility of starting afresh in a new place regardless of your emotional attachment to where you come from.

Do not be like frog B, who kept adjusting to the situation around him until he lost his life in the process.

Give Yourself to Discipline

Discipline is your ability to identify your true goal and then push yourself beyond your comfort zone every day to act in line with activities that reflect that goal.

For example, if you have a goal to lose some weight and get in shape, you will have to control your nutrition and hit the gym at least 5 or 6 days a week, regardless of what the weather looks like or if you don't feel like it.

Discipline requires you to diligently follow up with important tasks related to your goals every day. Never let a day go by without doing something that closes the gap between you and your target.

Lack of discipline is the reason why people don't excel in life. They are unable to discipline themselves to put in the effort over an extended period of time.

Deal with Your Fears

To deal with your fears, you need courage.
Courage is a state of mind that compels you to face
difficult situations in spite of fear.

Courage is not the absence of fear but the ability to
do what frightens you. That is, taking action in the
face of your fears.

It is the ability to act on your beliefs despite other
people's disproval and discouragement.

Although courage is not the absence of fear, the
absence of courage creates room for fear.

Contrary to popular belief, fear is not an abnormal
or bad thing. It is just another one of the many
emotions we feel in our lives.

If you analyze and break it down, you would see
that it is just what it is, *F.E.A.R*, false experiences
appearing real.

The fear I'm talking about here is not what you
feel when in the face of danger, like having a gun
pointed at you or in any other near-death
situation.

I am talking about that false story that you have
constantly fed your mind about something bad
that might happen in the future. I am talking about

the feeling that you are not good enough or qualified enough to assume full capacity.

Fear ought to be a fuel and a catalyst that should propel you into action.

Fear will keep you on the edge of your greatness waiting for that perfect moment that will never come.

As an actor, I have had the privilege of working on the same set with some big Hollywood names and pop stars like William Shatner, Cardi B, T.I, Chance The Rapper, Sean Kingston, just to mention a few.

One thing I noticed about every one of these stars is that they are very shy people. When the lights and cameras are not focused on them, they can hardly hold your stare when you look them in the eye.

However, check them out once the spotlight is on them. You see them tune into their element. You will see them literally switch from the shy-girl, shy-boy persona into full stage wonders.

People who society perceives to be courageous are simply the way they are, not because they do not feel afraid, but because they did what they ought to do in the face of their fears.

The point I'm trying to make is that your fear is normal. You are not alone. Everybody feels the same fear you feel but the question is what do you do about it? Do you allow it hold you back or make it your springboard for leaping higher?

Always Do More Than You Are Paid For

I remember the one time my wife and I had bought into a cable subscription that turned out to be different from what the cable company offered in their marketing commercial.

Dissatisfied, we decided to unsubscribe from their service and return the decoder they had issued us.

So, the company sends their tech guy over to come retrieve the item. The technician shows up, a very energetic fellow who sounded like he proliferates a thousand words per minute.

I thought I could convey my frustrations with their service to him, but he just point-blank told me that I'm talking to the wrong person. He asked that I direct all my complaints to the marketing department because there was nothing he could do about it. "I'm just the tech guy," he said with a slight shrug of his shoulders.

I felt a ding sound go off in my head. Every attempt I made to talk to him hit a brick wall. He just wouldn't listen to anything I was going to say.

Ordinarily, to any other person there was nothing wrong with his response or attitude, but to me this was the height of unprofessionalism and nonchalance toward company growth.

Why do I think so? Deflecting me to the marketing department, not only portrays him as selfish, it also showed that he lacks team-playing abilities and is indisposed to the growth of the company. If I were his employer, he would lose his job right there on the spot.

I believe that being the guy in the field on behalf of the company ought to put him in the best position to understand what the needs and concerns of the company's customers are, but he didn't care. He lacked the basic understanding of what customer acquisition and retention means to company growth.

If I were in his position as a field operations officer, I would interact with as many customers as possible, especially the disgruntled ones, take in whatever complaints and concerns they have raised and on my own come up with a solution to those issues raised in the form of a marketing plan, which I would go present to the most senior manager or CEO of the company.

The dream and vision of every director or CEO is to see their company grow. If I presented him or her with a solution plan like the one I had formulated, they would take me very seriously.

If I don't get a promotion sooner, I definitely would later. So my advice to you is that you always should be ready to do more than you are paid for because you never know who is watching or what you might learn in the process of doing so.

Never Underestimate What It Will Take

Understand that it's not going to be easy, especially in the beginning. There will be days you wake up wondering if you are doing the right thing.

There will be days when economic challenges, competition, and fear of failure will seem to overwhelm you.

There will also be days when the mockery and taunting of people around you will almost get to you.

You just have to understand that the world is filled with people who don't amount to much and yet are always ready to tear down people like you who dare to make smart moves and take concrete steps toward the right actions.

There is nothing they will throw at you that has not been seen or heard before by great achievers before you.

History is replete with stories of how the inventors of the great products and ideas we enjoy today were mocked and laughed at in scorn during their initial stages of development.

Remember, it pays to be bold and consistent, with your eyes focused on the finish line of the future.

So keep showing up, stay visible, and don't be afraid to raise your expectations

CHAPTER TEN

THE FOURTH DIMENSION

There's no better way to conclude this masterpiece than reserving the best and most important for the last.

The fourth dimension is the supernatural aspect of our being as it relates with the Creator of the universe.

Despite all we are, who we are, and what we know, there's a need to create a space for God in our lives by developing and sustaining a relationship with Him.

Creating a space for God simply means being all you can be in excellence yet allowing Him to manifest Himself in your life by acknowledging him as your source.

Everything we have mentioned in the previous chapters are great tactics and strategies but the truth is that anybody can be all that.

One thing that will set you apart from the pack is your deep conviction of the fact that the supernatural controls the physical.

For example, it is possible to attend all the trainings, have all the expert information, the skills and expertise, but if you don't have sound health that only comes from God, all of that comes to nullity.

Acknowledgement of the fourth dimension can be expressed by engaging in activities of faith, prayer, and thanksgiving.

Faith

Faith is the substance of things hoped for, the evidence of the things not yet seen.
Faith, though invisible, is a very powerful force.

No matter who you are in life, your faith will surely be tested; it is especially tested when life's challenges occur.

Challenge as a word here means different things to different people, as each and every one of us experience our challenges in various forms.

For some, it may come in the form of health challenge, for some others in the form of financial challenge, family challenge, relationship challenge, doubters challenge, time challenge, and fear challenge.

When all of these challenges occur, the one thing that will keep you going is your faith. That light of hope shining from within with the assurance that you will get through your dark moments.

Faith to a believer is what currency is to a businessman. God is very pleased with faith because without faith it is impossible to please or acknowledge Him. You need to keep in mind that every time you go through tough times, the one thing you cannot afford to lose is your faith.

Faith can be exercised in many forms. Prayers, thanksgiving, action and words are but a few ways through which your faith is expressed.

Prayer

Prayer is one of the greatest acts or displays of faith. How do you talk to someone you cannot see? It is a mystery yet a very potent force you can deploy whenever you feel stuck and confused.

Prayer is God's gift to mankind to access His presence in times of need. So feel free to seek help and direction whenever the need arises. Just as food nourishes the body, prayer nourishes the human soul and spirit.

The same way you can never eat enough food to last you long enough and therefore have to eat food every day, sometimes, three times a day to stay alive, so should your prayer life be.

Men and women ought to always pray.

Thanksgiving

Thanksgiving is the act of being grateful for the things you have while you await the things you don't have yet.
It is expressing appreciation to your Creator for giving you the chance to come into this world with a purpose to leave a mark in the sands of time.

Conclusion

As you go out there, my desire for you in all sincerity is that you will not only digest the mental weapons you have downloaded from this book but also be willing to deploy them in the battlefields of life.
.

May the changes and the great results you seek in life happen speedily for you.

ACKNOWLEDGEMENT

I want to specially thank God almighty for the grace and inspiration of putting pen to paper.

A very special thank you to all of the great men and women, far and near, some living and some resting with the Lord. Dr. Miles Monroe, Dr. Jim Rohn, Pastor Matthew Ashimolowo, Dr. Joyce Meyer, Steve Harvey and so many others who space will not permit me to mention. Under your tutelage, your teachings and exemplary lifestyle, my life took a drastic turnaround for good because I put to practice the things you taught me.

And to every one who purchased this book, may everything you have learnt on here bring you extraordinary results you'd surely be proud of and may the Lord bless you richly in Jesus' name.

ABOUT THE AUTHOR

Ugo Maduka is a prolific speaker, best-selling author and a passionate lover of God. He holds a degree in Education and is a certified life coach.
He is the founder and CEO of The Transformed Life Inc. Los Angeles, California.
Mount Up Your Wings is the first of his various publications series.
He is married to Amarachi Odinma-Maduka and thcy are blessed with two wonderful children .

www.ingramcontent.com/pod-product-compliance
Lightning Source LLC
Chambersburg PA
CBHW070339220526
45467CB00001B/172